LIFE AND DESTINY

By
FELIX ADLER

AMERICAN ETHICAL UNION
Two West 64th Street New York, N. Y. 10023

"Life and Destiny" by Felix Adler. ISBN 978-0-9897323-2-1.

Published by The American Ethical Union ©2013. All rights reserved. No part of this publication may be reproduced, stored in a retrieval system, or transmitted in any form or by any means, electronic, mechanical, recording or otherwise, without the prior written permission of The American Ethical Union.

Manufactured in the United States of America.

It is more than seventy years since Mrs. Felix Adler made these selections from addresses by Dr. Adler on Ethical Religion. Since its first publication this collection has been reissued several times, both in this country and in England.

In response to continued demand, the American Ethical Union, now offers it in the present form as part of the Hundreth Anniversary celebration of the Ethical Movement.

* * *

Horace L. Friess, Leader Emeritus of the New York Society for Ethical Culture and Professor Emeritus of Philosophy at Columbia University, has written a special introduction.

CONTENTS

INTRODUCTION 5

THE MEANING OF LIFE 17

RELIGION 23

IMMORTALITY 29

MORAL IDEALS 31

LOVE AND MARRIAGE 39

HIGHER LIFE 45

SPIRITUAL PROGRESS 53

SUFFERING AND CONSOLATION 56

ETHICAL OUTLOOK 63

INTRODUCTION

THIS little volume, first published in 1903, is composed of short quotations from the lectures of Felix Adler for the New York Society for Ethical Culture in its earlier years. The period covered by the selections is from- the founding of the Society in 1876 to 1902. In those years Felix Adler was in the thick of action and took hold of life with both hands. After university studies abroad he had felt it necessary to leave the Jewish ministry, but he always retained the Hebraic emphasis on ethical conduct and community in his sense of life. He also remained an essentially religious moralist, who struck a deep and authentic spiritual note.

He was born in 1851, and first came to this country with his parents and his older brother in 1857. His father, the Rev. Samuel Adler, was coming from western Germany to accept a post as rabbi at the Temple Emanu-El in New York. He was a man of remarkable self-discipline, excellent scholarship, and pronounced democratic tendencies. It was indeed a stirring baptism into American nationality which the family received soon after their arrival, when the storm of civil war broke upon the country. Later in life Felix Adler used to say that, in the teaching of American history, "the liberation of the slaves should be treated as the starting-point for the social mission of the American Republic." Certainly it was the starting-point of his own personal consciousness of American social and political ideals. The nation's standard, as he saw it, was established in. that struggle.

After graduating from Columbia College in 1870, Felix Adler spent three years as a university student on the Continent; principally in Berlin, though he received his Ph. D. in

Semitics from Heidelberg in 1873. Europe was violently and dramatically stirred in those years by issues of nationalism, clericalism, and by "the social question" of class relationships in modern industrial society. It was also a time of profound intellectual change in the study of man, when history, anthropology, and doctrines of biological evolution were introducing fundamentally new views of human development. Returning to America, at the age of twenty-two, young Dr. Adler discovered that he could no longer find his calling in the rabbinic office which his father and generations of earlier forbears had served. For three years he taught Hebrew and Oriental Literature at Cornell University. But his sense that the core of life, and of religion, is moral and practical did not allow him to be just the scholar. In that post-war era of expanding industrial ambitions, the "uproarious tide" of American life both challenged and depressed him. From the influence of Emerson, Parker, and their circles in New England he took hope that a moral and spiritual expansion was also possible in this land.

Adler now attended meetings of the Free Religious Association, a development among liberal Unitarians and others, more interested in open search for religious truth than in defending "the legacy of theological tradition." Indeed, subsequently, from 1878 to 1882, he became the President of this Association. But this was after he had come before the public as a "religious radical" by founding the New York Society for Ethical Culture in 1876.

Dr. Adler described the current on which he and his followers launched the Ethical Culture Movement as follows:

> We saw that the great tides of being are everywhere sweeping mankind on to larger achievements than were known to the past; only within the churches all is still and motionless; only within the churches the obsolete forms of centuries ago are retained, or if concessions to the present are made, they are tardy, ungracious and insufficient. We beheld that the essentials of religion are neglected, even while its accessories are observed with greater punctiliousness than ever.

Despite this sharp criticism of the churches, Adler was not interested in engaging in primarily negative iconoclasm. He declared that he "never was an atheist." In his student years he had lost the traditional belief in a single, personal God who hears prayers, and thereafter he arrived at another conception of Godhead only gradually and with maturity. But throughout life he consistently affirmed a transcendent, "Divine source of the Moral Law."

Adler fervently wanted religion to move constructively like other great tides of the age. But, in this very interest, he thought that Ethical Culture should not make a binding standard of his own or any other religious beliefs. Instead, he thought it vital that people of different outlooks, both. religious and secular, should unite in the Movement's essential work of forwarding a greater moral community. At no time has the membership been required to subscribe to a religious creed. This undogmatic basis of fellowship, Adler thought, would promise most for future spiritual progress, agreeable to human variety, to scientific mentality, and to the universal claims of morality.

"Deed before creed" was for a time the watchword of the new Society for Ethical Culture. Felix Adler was disappointed to find the Free Religious Association so purely speculative and theoretical in its approach to religion. "One cannot attain religion merely by trying, in his closet, to think out the problems of the universe," he told his own followers. And while he instructed them from Sunday to Sunday, with philosophical understanding, he also led them in a great program of work to be done. He had a marked ability to interpret the connection between next steps that every man could take and the more far-reaching issues of thought and culture that spanned the centuries.

There were critics, especially in Jewish circles, who predicted that Felix Adler, having broken the traces of established religion, would soon be found grazing on the flatlands of social work and simple philanthropy. The tolerance of secularists in his Society, and the activities launched there, might suggest this criticism to a superficial view. But it was not discerning of Dr. Adler's own interest, which in all his efforts remained basically religious. No so much the reforms *per se,* but rather the effect of the effort upon men's conceptions of themselves and their role in the world concerned him. He saw the limited results of all reforming activity even at best. But he believed that persistent effort in right directions could yield a vision and a sense of man's participation in the Divine life of the world. And this to him was the supreme boon. Moreover, with growing knowledge of human frailty, the need of sustaining spiritual discipline and of vision transcending frustration was born in upon him. In the sentences of *Life and Destiny* his religious response to life's pain has not found its final and most mature expression. He appeals here, without much interpretation, to a rather plain "religion of duty." The severe note of commanding resolution to carry on amid all difficulties runs through these sentences like a cord of iron.

The program of action which Adler set before his Society, beginning in its second year, included the following measures: he wanted to establish free kindergartens to take the young children of working people out of crowded tenements and streets and give them a more wholesome start in life. Beyond that he wanted the public schools to adopt new measures of manual training and "industrial education uniting hand and brain." He wanted to develop the education of women to make them more intelligent mothers and more complete companions of their husbands. For the moral and emotional development of the young he wanted also to launch a non-dogmatic type of ethical and religious instruction. He wanted to send visiting nurses and medicines, free of charge, into the homes of the sick poor. He wanted to foster cooperative industries. He wanted to relieve congestion in cities by "colonizing" rural areas on a cooperative community basis. His immediate efforts in the last two directions were not permanently successful. But the schools and organizations started by Felix Adler and his followers to further the other objectives all bore lasting and valuable fruit. Moreover, as early as 1880, he advocated that a system of graduated income and inheritance taxes should be instituted to enable government to advance similar measures, especially in the educational field, on a wide scale.

At this point some newspapers attacked Adler for preaching "communistic sermons." The fact is that he did mean definitely to break with laisser-faire individualism. Indeed, he called individualism "the chief evil of the age" in morals and in religion no less than in politics. He predicted that democracy must either perish of it, or else appropriately "organize" itself. But during the '80's and '90's Felix Adler also made dear that he did not see the promise of such organization in current philosophies of socialism. He criticized not only the materialistic premises, but also the single-tracked economic prescriptions of Marxian doctrine. Its collectivism seemed to him that of a mass or aggregate of individuals conceived as economic men. He did not believe such a mass could hold together except under enormous authoritarian pressures.

In contrast both to individualism and such collectivism Felix Adler worked to advance a third alternative which he sometimes called the idea of "organized democracy." Organization should be valued, he said, as essential to the development of a democratic community of free, creative personalities, but also criticized in terms of what is required for such development. Free men are nevertheless interdependent, and come into being through a series of essential relationships in the family, school, vocation, state, and religious fellowship. An ethical view of society cannot grant an absolute sovereignty to any of these relations, but must accord the authority to each required for its specific functions. Moreover, each relation both serves and depends upon the others for its own proper fulfillment. With this outlook, Dr. Adler could not place confidence in any single-tracked reform or panacea. Necessarily he relied on, and worked for, the interlinking of constructive measures in each of the main relations of life.

A striking singleness of purpose, however, unified his long career of many-sided activity. In all he did he worked to advance the sense that "we live truly in our radiations." "We grow and develop in proportion as we help others to grow and develop." His ethical principle was one neither of egoism nor altruism, but rather of "joint development" through mutual interplay.

In the interest of strengthening family life, Dr. Adler became a zealous crusader in the early '80's for better city housing, and served on the Tenement House Commission. He also fought with several citizens' committees against vice in the tenements. He severely criticized individualistic views of marriage as a factor in the rising divorce rate. He sought to reinterpret and to reaffirm the social ends of marriage, but in the spirit of democratic ideals of freedom and equality. He believed that broader education and roles for women could be shaped to strengthen, rather than to weaken, family relations. He wanted mothers to cultivate enlightened child study.

He made an early inquiry and attack, in 1887, on child labor, and became Chairman subsequently and for many years of the National Child Labor Committee. In the Kindergarten and the School, which he had founded, he sought to demonstrate methods of education favoring a "larger humanity in the young." Medical care, parent participation, links between school and community, a broader program of arts and crafts, of history, science, and language study took the place of mechanical drill in the three r's. Speaking of Adler's school in 1891, President Hunt of the New York City Board of Education said: "If I could have my way, every Public School in this city would be conducted in accordance with the system of instruction adopted in this school." And as a matter of fact, the Ethical Culture School was one that led a way in the great expansion of American public education which has taken place in the last fifty years.

In 1885, Felix Adler publicly supported Henry George in his campaign to become Mayor of New York. It was not, he explained, because he believed in the single tax, but because George put forward the cause of labor as a political issue. Adler believed that political gains would come from the facing of new issues, and above all that of "the liberation of labor." The theory and method of that liberation had indeed become a prime issue. In 1891, Dr. Adler joined a number of scholars and civic workers in establishing a summer school at Plymouth, where the ethics of "the labor question" was discussed as being "the chief moral question of the day" in that it affected all others. As Professor of Social and Political Ethics at Columbia University, from 1903 until his death in 1933, he continued to discuss the ethics of this and other social questions with university and seminary students over many years.

Dr. Adler was prepared to give large support to the program of organized labor, as a necessary instrument under competitive conditions for regulating the right to work. To secure the conditions for doing one's work well, and to achieve the human dignity which that implies, should be labor's dominant objective, he urged. Ultimately Felix Adler looked beyond the prevailing system of competitive business with its concomitant of collective bargaining by labor unions exercising the right to strike. He envisaged the coming of a more cooperative system, with some industries organized by government and others by guilds of workers choosing and employing their own managers. But despite the fact that he contemplated such truly radical changes, Dr. Adler was the opposite of impatient. The balance and comprehensiveness of his judgment was recognized on both sides of the industrial struggle, and won confidence in him as a fairly arbitrating and wisely counseling fellow-citizen.

The twentieth century opened with what Adler took to be signs of a gathering international crisis. The Boer War and the United States conquest of the Philippines impressed him and many other liberals as ominous portents. The great democracies, no less than other states, were being drawn into a deepening vortex of imperialistic rivalries. When World War I broke upon an astonished world Felix Adler saw it primarily in these terms. He could not agree that it was really "to make the world safe for democracy." In order for international law to supplant anarchy and war, a system would have to be devised to give nationalities legitimate protection and security. The gate to such a system might be found, he thought, in establishing international trusteeships for the weaker, less developed peoples of the earth. But as long as the great nations vied in exploiting the weak, they would fight amongst themselves. Dr. Adler believed that the growth of more peaceful international society could not be the work of governments alone, but must involve the meeting and collaboration of peoples in many kinds of "assemblies." As early as 1911, he had himself been the Chairman of a first World Races Congress convened in London.

Many concrete measures of social reform that had been part of Adler's program over the years were definitely advanced by the liberal movement in American politics, especially under the leadership of Woodrow Wilson and Franklin Roosevelt. Yet Dr. Adler remained a critic of the prevailing liberal philosophies. He found Wilson's conception of "the new freedom" and of "the self-determination of nations" still too individualistic. It emphasized the independence rather than the interdependence of individuals and of groups.

Moreover, for himself, Felix Adler was not content with any secular version of humanitarianism. Indeed, his central concern was to put striving for human betterment in a spiritual perspective, to give it a free religious interpretation independent of dogma and exclusive church control. He did not think of substituting political and social activity for religion. He well understood the inevitable inadequacy of political and social results to satisfy the ideal longings awakened in the human heart and spirit. But he did conceive that a new sense of perfection, of the Divine Life, could arise on the basis of thoroughgoing effort to expand the moral fellowship of men in all the relations of our world. He did not believe it could be the vision, predicted by St. Paul, of one God covering "all in all, as the waters cover the sea." It would have to be a sense of the Divine Life, not as one rolling sea, but as the differentiated symphonic interplay of each distinct person in an infinite host upon the others. In any case, it would be an experience arising out of fuller regard for diversity within community than did earlier religions.

Felix Adler sometimes spoke of his final theology as offering a "social conception of God." By that he did not mean to make a god of human society, not even when conceived as an ideal community. What he did hold was that community, in an ideal sense, can be a more adequate ethical symbol of the Divine than can an individual person. In line with this thought is the statement in *Life and Destiny* that: "The higher life—the germ of which exists in every man—is adequately represented by no man. The one represents more adequately some particular aspect of it, another a different aspect of it." But Adler's religious conception was not yet complete at the time of these sentences.

In his relation to the churches Felix Adler stood among the radically dissenting reformers. But he stood also within classic religion in many ways, and particularly in affirming an ultimate love as being of the divine in man. Though he held a distinctive version of that idea, it was in line with high tradition in several central respects. His conception continued the accent in classic religion upon the ultimate love as a power enduring and surmounting evil. It also emphasized the completely universal character of this divine love's ties, connecting every man one with another, and with an infinitely transcendent spiritual universe. A somewhat less traditional accent Adler put on the idea that each person lives in the others not only through likeness, but also through difference. Love extends to the unique, induplicable variation each essential self represents in the divine communion of all.

The wars and revolutions that surrounded his late years neither excited nor shook Dr. Adler's deep hope for eventual spiritual progress. From the wars he said he expected to see "more recrudescence of superstition than reawakening of religion." "Only in the longer reach of time does religious progress seem possible as a consequence of the long gathering forces that will make for a better adjustment between religion and other aspects of developing society, for the emergence of a differently and more broadly educated leadership in religion, and for the growing interplay of the earth's peoples and civilizations."

In his unshaken belief in the possibility of spiritual progress, Dr. Adler was no shallow optimist overlooking the tragic side of life. Not only his late writings, but also these earlier pages of *Life and Destiny* show how much he was concerned from the beginning to confront the darker facts of "sickness, sorrow, and sin." As early as 1880, however, he stated his conviction that the motive to achieve social progress would prove spiritually superior to traditional ways of "atonement" in meeting these very evils. The ideal of social progress is not only for fair weather, he said, but will help men bear adversity more fruitfully than mere stoicism or hope of after-life compensations. To this conviction Adler remained firmly attached. In contrast to those who. claim that political and social health depends on return to the old religious faiths, he committed his life and its work to the belief that "social and religious improvement must go together."

So frequently are the shadows and sufferings of life mentioned in Adler's pages, that it may even be necessary to point out that his thought does not rest with them. "We must press on through the darkness and the terror of it if we would reach the holier light beyond," he says in the opening sentences of *Life and Destiny*. And this is the key thought often repeated thereafter. "At bottom, the world is to be interpreted in terms of joy, but of a joy that includes all the pain, includes it and transforms it and transcends it. The Light of the World is a light that is saturated with the darkness which it has overcome and transfigured." "Religion faces the wreck of worlds, and prophesies restoration. She faces a sky blood-red with sunset colors that deepen into darkness, and prophesies dawn. She faces death, and prophesies life."

But Felix Adler was ever concerned that religion's restoring prophecy should not be one of murky mysticism or of soft escape from responsibilities. Instead his energetic ethical persuasion looked to spiritual perspectives of a sun-lit clarity for the renewal of human action. "The right course," he claimed, "must insure vigor of attack, a relish for the struggle of life, an attitude of interest in finite things, and a certain élan of spirit in grappling with the work-a-day world, if this line is to be followed, the business of life in all its branches, every one of its interests and activities, must be interpreted spiritually. Unless we see something precious, something ineffably worth while in our finite relations, the notion of the infinite itself will be empty of all content. A truer vision of the ideal can arise only on the basis of persistence and fortitude in grappling with actual circumstances throughout life."

•

AN INVITATION to membership in any of the Ethical Societies is extended to all who are in sympathy with their purposes and philosophy. No creed or fixed set of principles is submitted at any time. A simple application for membership is followed by the opportunity for personal interviews with one of the Leaders, when the significance of the ethical point of view and the opportunities within the Societies can be explained. The Societies are supported by voluntary contributions. Each member is expected to share in the responsibilities as well as in the privileges of the Societies and to give as generously as means will permit. Individual memberships are also welcomed in the American Ethical Union.

HORACE L. FRIESS

THE MEANING OF LIFE

THERE are two kinds of light, the light on the hither side of the darkness and the light beyond the darkness. We *must press on* through the darkness and the terror of it if we would reach the holier light beyond.

We are here—no matter who put us here, or how we came here—to fulfill a task. We cannot afford to go of our own volition until the last item of our duty is discharged. We are here to make mind master of matter, soul of sense. We do so by overriding pain, not by weakly capitulating to it.

When we are smitten by the rod of affliction, do not let us sit still, but rather get to work as fast as we can. In action lies our salvation. But it must be remembered that only a great aim, one which remains valid, irrespective of our private griefs, is competent in the critical moments to put us into action and to sustain us in action.

The thought that extreme suffering is a key which unlocks life's deepest and truest meanings is the final rejoinder to the plea on behalf of suicide. It is a thought which, when fully apprehended, is calculated to give peace to every troubled soul.

The fact that there is a spiritual power in us, that is to say, a power which testifies to the unity of our life with the life of others, which impels us to regard others as other selves—this fact comes home to us even more forcibly in sorrow than in joy. It is thrown into clearest relief on the background of pain.

In the glow of achievement we are apt to be full of a false self-importance. But in moments of weakness we realize, through contrast, the infinitely superior strength of the power whose very humble organs and ministers we are. It is then we come to understand that, isolated from it, we are nothing; at one with it, identified with it, we participate in its eternal nature, in its resistless course.

There are two terms of the series of progress which we should always keep before us. The one is the starting point, and the other the final goal. The former is the cave man: the latter is the divine man. We know in a measure what sort of being the cave man was. Instructed by anthropologists, we know how poor and mean were the beginnings of humanity on earth. But of that other term of progress—the goal of progress, the divine man of whom the cave man was the germ, the first rough draft of the man who is to be—our notions are vague. He rises before us, indeed, in a vision of glory, but his shape is nebulous. And the result of progress is just this, that it makes us more and more able to define the outlines of that shape, to draw sharply and finely the noble lineaments of that face; that it makes us more and more able to see the divine, the perfect man, the only begotten son of all the spirits of the myriads of the generations of men-—the man that is to be, the perfection of our imperfection.

THE MEANING OF LIFE

The perfect man has never yet appeared on earth. The perfect man is an apparition of light and beauty rising in the boundless infinite, an ideal to be more and more clothed with particularity. The purpose for which we exist is to help to create the perfect man, to incarnate him more and more in ourselves and in others.

That the lofty form of man may be wholly disengaged from the encompassing clay, that the traces of the first rough draft of the man who is to be—our nature, that our spirits may stand erect as our bodies already do—this, I think, is the end for which we exist.

Every man, however humble, is worthy of reverence because, in his limited sphere, he can be a beneficent, forward-working agent, he can help a little to create the perfect man. Every child is a possible avatar of the more perfect man. On every child the whole past lays its burdens, and of the outcome of its life the whole future is expectant.

The way to overcome dejection is to energise our nature vigorously. An eminent physician is quoted as saying: "I firmly believe that one-half of the confirmed invalids could be cured of their maladies if they were compelled to live busy and active lives, and had no time to fret over their miseries. The will has a wonderfully strong and direct influence over the body. Good work is the safeguard of health. The way to live well is to work well." If this be true, even when the cause of the dejection is corporeal, how much more likely it is to be true where the cause is seated in the mind.

LIFE AND DESTINY

In cases of bereavement, what is it that can enable a man to weather the hurricane of grief which is apt to descend upon the soul immediately after a great loss; and what can enable him to live through the dead calm which is apt to succeed that first whirlwind of passionate desolation? It is the thought that the fight must still go on, because there are issues of infinite worth at stake; and that, though wounded and crippled, he must still bear his part in the fight until the end.

For singleness of purpose, I plead. This alone can give strength to our will, coherence to our life. Without it we drift; with it we steer. Let us have before us, whatever we do, a sovereign aim, but let us also make sure that it be a worthy aim, one that will purge the clay from our eyes, from our lips, from our brains, from our hearts.

A great man helps us by the standard which he erects. He never really is level with his own standard, and yet we do not therefore reject him. He helps us by what he earnestly tries for, and by what he suggests to us that we should try for he helps us, not so much by what he achieves, as by what he reveals, by the insight which he gives us into the nature of good.

So far as the forward movement of the human race is concerned, it is the effort that counts, and not the attainment; the realm of time and space can never be the scene of complete realisation. The reward of the effort is the wider outlook upon the ultimate aim; the truer estimate of its character as infinite, and, along with this, the recognition of that infiniteness of our nature which enables us to conceive of and aspire to such an aim.

Joy is a light which those who possess are bound to keep burning brightly for the sake of others as well as for their own sake. Every pure joy in the world is so much pure gain.

Cold and bare is youth without the glow of generous idealism. Contemptible is middle age without the sense of definite attachments and the willing acceptance of limitations. And ungracious and unlovely is old age if it be not illumined by the light of contemplation, if it be not fruitful in counsel.

Every vocation, even the lowliest, which we pursue in a spirit of entire sincerity, is a means of acquiring culture. The artisan may be, in his way, as truly a cultivated man as the artist or the scholar, for by culture I understand insight gained into all manner of activities through genuineness and thoroughness in one. To be cultivated is to see things in their relations.

Our daily avocation, whatever it be, if we cling to it closely enough, is sure to engender in us a new respect for reality, a new humility.

To put forth power in such a way as to be provocative of power in others is the ethical aim that should guide men in all vocations and in all their relations.

This fair earth, with its fir-clad hills, its snowy mountains, its sparkling seas, its azure vaults, and the holy light of the stars, is but a painted screen behind which lurks the true reality.

LIFE AND DESTINY

The beauty of this earth and all that is precious and great in this human life of ours is but a hint and a suggestion of an eternal fairness, an eternal rightness.

We need something of the virility of Stoicism to grapple with the difficulties of life; we need to cultivate a large patience; an humble spirit that teaches us to be prepared for every loss, and to welcome every joy as an unlooked-for gain. There are a thousand pleasures in little things which we, with the petulance of children, daily spurn, because we cannot have all we ask for.

The question, Is life worth living? implies a species of blasphemy. The right question to ask is: Am I worthy of living? If I am not, I can make myself so. That is always in my power.

At bottom, the world is to be interpreted in terms of joy, but of a joy that includes all the pain, includes it and transforms it and transcends it.

The Light of the World is a light that is saturated with the darkness which it has overcome and transfigured.

RELIGION

RELIGION is a wizard, a sibyl. She faces the wreck of worlds, and prophesies restoration. She faces a sky blood-red with sunset colours that deepen into darkness, and prophesies dawn. She faces death, and prophesies life.

Religion has been so eager to supply us with information concerning the universe outside of us, its origin and its destiny, because our life is linked with that of the universe, and our destiny is dependent on the destiny of the universe.

The dependence of man on outside forces which he cannot control is the point of departure of religion.

It is the moral element contained in it that alone gives value and dignity to a religion, and only in so far as its teachings serve to stimulate and purify our moral aspirations does it deserve to retain its ascendency over mankind.

"There is a time to act for the Lord by breaking his commandments" was a saying current among the ancient Hebrews. This means there is a time to act for religion by protesting against what passes for religion; there is a time to prepare the way for a larger morality by shattering the narrow forms of dogma whereby the progress of morality is hindered.

LIFE AND DESTINY

Ethical religion can be real only to those who are engaged in ceaseless efforts at moral improvement. By moving upward we acquire faith in an upward movement, without limit.

The symbols of religion are ciphers of which the key is to be found in moral experience. It is in vain we pore over the ciphers unless we possess the key.

To understand the meaning of a great religious teacher we must find in our own life experiences somewhat akin to his. To selfish, unprincipled persons whose hearts are wholly set on worldly ends, what meaning, for instance, can such utterances have as these? "You must become like little children if you would possess the kingdom of heaven;" "You must be willing to lose your life in order to save it;" "If you would be first you must consent to be last." To the worldly-minded such words convey no sense whatever; they are, in fact, rank absurdity.

Of the origin of things we know nothing, and can know nothing. Perfection does not reveal itself to us as existent in the beginning; but as something that ought to be, something new which we are to help create. Somehow the secret of the universe is hidden in our breast. Somehow the destinies of the universe depend upon our exertions.

The infinite, from which comes the impulse that leads us to activity, is not the highest Reason, but higher than reason; not the highest Goodness, but higher than goodness.

There is a city to be built, the plan of which we

RELIGION

carry in our heads, in our hearts. Countless generations have already toiled at the building of it. The effort to aid in completing it takes, with us, the place of prayer. In this sense we say, *"Laborare est orare."*

The essential faith is the product of effort and is sustained and clarified by effort.

What is the way to get a religion? We know, at all events, what cannot be the way. It cannot be to prostrate our intellects before the throne of authority; to bind the Samson within us, the human mind, and deliver him into the hands of the Philistines; to abjure our reason. Whatever religion we adopt must be consistent with the truth with which we have been enriched at the hands of science. It may be ultra-scientific —indeed, it must be; but it may not be anti-scientific.

But, on the other hand, we need to be equally warned against expecting too much from the intellect. One cannot attain religion merely by trying, in his closet, to think out the problem of the universe.

It is a mistake to approach the subject of religion from the point of view of philosophy. All really religious persons declare that religion is, primarily, a matter of experience. We must get a certain kind of experience, and then philosophic thinking will be of use to us in explicating what is implicated in that experience. But we must get the experience first.

The undulatory theory would not help anyone to know what light is who had never seen light, and the chemical formula for water would not help any one to know what water is who had never tasted it.

LIFE AND DESTINY

To know light one must see it; to know water one must taste it. So, too, philosophy will not help any one to know what religion is.

The experience of religion is not reserved for the initiated and elect, it is accessible to everyone who chooses to have it.

The experience to which I refer is essentially moral" experience. It may be described as a sense of subjection to imperious impulses which urge our finite nature toward infinite issues; a sense of propulsions which we can resist, but not disown; a sense of a power greater than ourselves, with which, nevertheless, in essence we are one; a sense, in times of moral stress, of channels opened by persistent effort, which let in a flood of rejuvenating energy and put us in command of unsuspected moral resources; a sense, finally, of the complicity of our life with the life of others, of living in them in no merely metaphorical signification of the word; of unity with all spiritual being whatsoever.

A religion which is to satisfy us must be a religion of progress. But we must be progressive ourselves if we are to have faith in progress. We must be constantly developing if we are to have faith in unbounded further development. And especially we must be progressing in a moral direction.

We should acquire the habit of taking stock from time to time of our moral possessions, of keeping faithful count of our net gains and losses. Do we, for instance, possess more fortitude, or less, in encountering

RELIGION

unavoidable pain? Are we in better or worse control of our passions, of our tempers? Alas, that many of us, as we grow older, become more fretful and irascible, a greater trial and burden to our surroundings. Are we more broadly charitable in our judgment of others; more ready to make allowance for their faults, to bear with their shortcomings? Are we more or are we less devoted to the public ends of humanity? Does our idealism turn out to have been a mere ebullition of optimistic youth, a mere flash in the pan? Or does it grow wiser and warmer with the years? Does it burn with a steadier glow? Are we learning resignation, renunciation? It is by an honest answer given to such questions as these that; we may decide whether we are progressing or retrograding.

When we have reached a certain stage of culture, genuine gratitude and the verbal expression of it are inconsistent. We can say thanks for the little gifts, the lesser favours. But when the gift is great, and the debt exceedingly heavy, when we are full to overflowing with gratitude, then the words die upon our lips, and the only way to show our gratitude is by the use we make of the benefits we receive. For this reason, among others, the verbal expression of thanks to the Infinite Being in the form of prayer has always seemed to me a kind of desecration.

Because the Hebrew view of life is essentially the ethical view, therefore we still go back to the writings in which this view was first promulgated, and delight in them, as we do in no other scriptures in the world.

All of us are spiritually the heirs of the Hebrew

prophets, including among them Jesus, the greatest of their number.

There are moral traits in all religions, but, as a rule, they are subordinated. Morality is subordinated to *beauty* and *harmony* in the Greek ideal. It is the accompaniment and consequence of *order* in the Confucian scheme. It is but one form of the *brightness* of things, as opposed to darkness and evil, in Zoroastrianism. But to the Hebrew thought, moral excellence is the supreme excellence to which every other species of excellence is tributary.

The Hebrew religion and its descendants are the only ethical religions, strictly speaking, because in the Hebrew religion the moral element is constitutive and sovereign.

That the moral "ought" cannot be explained as the product of physical causation, is the greatest contribution which the Hebrew people have made to the religious and moral history of mankind.

A new Easter Day will come for mankind, when a race of religious teachers shall arise, who will be consecrated for their work by a more adequate training and a deeper moral enthusiasm, whose word will again be mighty as of old to inform the conscience of nations, and who shall carry the glad tidings of a higher life to the ends of the earth.

IMMORTALITY

THE dead are not dead if we have loved them truly. In our own lives we can give them a kind of immortality. Let us arise and take up the work they have left unfinished, and preserve intact the treasures they have won, and round out, if possible, the circuit of their being to the fullness of an ampler orbit in our own.

They that have left us are not afar; their presence is near and real, a silent and august companionship. In still hours of meditation, in the stress of action, in the midst of trials and temptations, we hear their voices whispering words of cheer or warning, and our deeds are, in a sense, their deeds, and our lives their lives.

So does the light of other days still shine in the bright-hued flowers that clothe our fields. So do they who have long since been gathered into the silent city of the dead still live in the deeds we do for their sake, in the earnest effort we put forth toward greater rectitude, patience, purity, under the influence of their unforgettable memories.

The conservation of moral energy is in a certain sense as true as the conservation of mechanical energy. We are not dust merely that returns to dust; we are not summer flies that bask in the sunshine of a passing day; we are not bounded in our influence by the narrow boundary of our years.]

LIFE AND DESTINY

In aspiring to noble ends, the soul takes on something of the greatness of that which it truly admires.

The evident disparity between virtue and happiness has led men to take refuge in the thought of compensation hereafter, and the necessity of a future state in which the good shall be rewarded and the evil punished has been deduced from the very inequities and moral inconsistencies of our present experience. The argument in this specific form is worthless, but it is based, nevertheless, upon a capital truth—the truth, namely, that our moral ideal is destined to be realised, though we may not know *how* it will be realised.

Vast possibilities suggest themselves to us of an order of existence wholly different from all that we have ever known; a gleam reaches the eye, as it were, from a far celestial land, and the crimson dawn of a Sun of Truth appears, to which the splendours of our earthly mornings are as obscurity.

MORAL IDEALS

AS the light of morning strikes now one peak and then another, some being illuminated while others are in the shadow, so the light of the essential moral principle shines now upon one duty and then upon another, while others are in the shadow.

Let us religiously set apart times and seasons in which to gather up the fruits of action and to experience the reactions which should follow on action. The most valuable of these fruits is just the intensified appreciation of the disparity existing between our achievements and the goal, the clearer vision of the goal, the sublimer and truer conception of it.

In order to join vigorously in the moral work of the world I must believe that somehow the best I can accomplish will endure, will leave its trace on things, will aid the final consummation.

What is needed above all else, is to find a more secure basis for morality, now that the theological basis has slipped away; to rekindle the belief in the ideal,-to bring into new prominence the unchanging truths, and to discover the new truths which men need for their moral guidance.

It is said that we live in order to make the world better, but this phrase is ambiguous. Often it is used as referring merely to an increase of the sum of human pleasure. And this would be an aim by no means comparable in grandeur and sublimity to that which religion in the past has set up.

We live to unfold the unmanifested potentialities of the universe, so far as they are latent in man, who, as far as we know, is the highest product of the universe. We live to enhance mentality and morality in the world. A developed mentality and morality will of itself cure the evils of poverty, and ignorance and sin. It may bring pleasure in its train, or may not bring it —it matters not. Not the fool's paradise of ease and enjoyment, but the heightened mentality and morality is the aim.

The moral ideal in its simplicity is all-sufficient. Its native charm can derive no added splendour from the drapery of creeds. Its severe beauty needs no factitious embellishment of myth and legend. The conviction that this is so has long been cherished by solitary thinkers. We should endeavour to spread it among the people. We should seek to lift it into the clear light of consciousness as the one commanding end of human endeavor, the supreme object of reverence and devotion.

Day by day there are triumphs to be won over the passion that stirs in our breasts; over the rising anger that sears our lips; over the turpitudes that defile our hearts; over the spirit of impatience and mutiny that threatens the authority of our reason. By such triumphs we are raised above our baser selves, and the fire which consumes our grosser natures, like the flaming chariot of Elijah, bears us living into a higher world.

To those who take part with all their heart and all their might in the struggle, there comes, at last, a great peace, a purified gladness. Gladness, in some instances, springs from a natural buoyancy of temperament, and is quite consistent with shallowness and superficiality of character. In other cases it is coincident with the swift flow of the currents of the blood, and ceases when the stream flows more slowly and begins to stagnate. Or it is due to gifts which an exceptional good fortune showers into the laps of favoured mortals. Gladness of this sort comes with happiness and departs with it.

But the purified gladness of which I speak is not dependent on these accidents. It is the mark of the ripest wisdom, and is based on the conviction, gained through experience, that life is worth living, that the victory is assured, and that the ends we pursue are of such excellence as to be incapable of ultimate defeat.

The moral ideal would embrace the whole of life. In its sight nothing is petty or indifferent. It touches the veriest trifles and turns them into shining gold. We are royal by virtue of it, and like the kings in the fair tale, we may never lay aside our crowns.

The moral order never is, but is ever becoming. It grows with our growth.

We call him a hero who maintains himself, single-handed, against superior numbers. We call him a master-horseman who sits a fiery and vicious steed,

LIFE AND DESTINY

guiding him at will. And in like manner, we call him a moral hero who conquers the enemies within his own breast—and we admire and revere the soul which can ride its own passions and force them into obedience to the dictates of reason.

The legend of St. Christopher, who undertook to carry the Christ-child on his shoulders across a stream, is applicable in a wider sense to us all. The deeper he entered into the water the heavier became the burden which he had assumed so lightly in the beginning, until it pressed upon him like a mountain, and he threatened to succumb beneath its weight. Such likewise is the case of him who, in the sanguine days of youth, has assumed the moral task of reforming himself, or others. The deeper he enters into the stream of life the heavier becomes the burden, and there is no salvation for him unless his strength increases in proportion as the load increases.

Do not court temptation. You cannot know whether you will be strong enough to resist it. But prepare yourself to deal valiantly with those temptations that are sure to come to you unsought, especially if you are a "live" man.

The marks of evil upon the soul are like the lines left by the glaciers of the ice-age on the ancient rocks. The glaciers have retreated, the ice-age has gone, a warmer climate has succeeded, but the marks remain.

Morality does not mope in corners, is not sour or gloomy. It loves to convert our meanest wants into golden occasions for fellowship and happy communion.

MORAL IDEALS

The moral ideal seeks to influence and interpenetrate the most ordinary affairs of private life.

The moral view of politics teaches us to hold the idea of country superior to the utilities of party, to exact worthiness of public servants, and to place the common good above the interests of particular classes.

The moral view of commerce bids the merchant put conscience into his wares and dealings and keep steadily in sight the larger purposes of human welfare.

The moral view of the professions leads their representatives to subordinate the claims of ambition and of material gain to the enduring interests of science, of justice, and to all the permanent social interests that are confided to their keeping.

The purpose of man's life is not happiness, but worthiness. Happiness may come as an accessory; we dare never make it the end.

We shall find men who are in the best sense successful in the miserable tenements of the poor.

An exalted type of morality is achieved by him who renounces in spirit the opportunities which he lacks, who accepts his limitations, and who, under the most trying circumstances, does not remit his efforts, no matter how insignificant may be their result, to promote the good.

An exalted type of morality is displayed by aged men who, with weakened frames and energies impaired, are yet resolved to die in harness.

An exalted type of morality is displayed by those who, cut off from the opportunities of culture, and from

LIFE AND DESTINY

most of the pleasures and comforts of existence, yet nourish, under the ashes of disappointed hopes, the feeblest remaining spark of the spiritual life, because they believe it to be a spark from an imperishable fire, even from that undying flame which burns at the heart of things, and which is destined to grow brighter and brighter as time rolls on.

There was once a teacher who had many pupils. Some of these he placed in a garden and bade them cultivate flowers, and said to them: "Fail not to bring your fairest flowers to me." But they became so much absorbed in the delights of the garden, as to forget entirely the master who had placed them there.

Others of his pupils he admitted to his library, and gave them access to many volumes rich in learning, and bade them ponder these stores of wisdom and bring the fruit of their reflections to him. But they also became wholly engrossed in their occupations.

And, again, there was a third company of pupils, whom he selected to be the dispensers of the hospitalities of his household. He bade them preside over his feasts, and entertain the guests as they arrive—"Only forget not," he said, "to bring the guests at last to me." But these, too, became wholly interested in their pleasures, and forgot the master and his charge.

But there were other pupils, whom, for an inscrutable reason, the master appointed to the hardest sort of service. He made them doorkeepers to admit others into the festive halls, while they themselves were compelled to remain without in the cold. He commanded

MORAL IDEALS

them to be hewers of wood and drawers of water, and to carry heavy burdens all day long. But, behold these poor drudges constantly thought of him. The very repulsiveness of their tasks made them think of him. Loyalty to their master alone kept them faithful to their tasks. And so those who seemed at the greatest distance from him were really nearest to him in their thoughts. They could bring him, it is true, neither flower nor book, they could only tell him of |he heavy loads they had borne, of the hard labour they had performed in the service of his entire household, and of their implicit obedience to his will.

In the great Academies of the Middle Ages there were four faculties, from at least one of which a student must graduate before he could claim the title of Doctor, or "Learned One." So likewise in the great university of life there are four faculties, each having at its head a great professor. The name of one professor is Poverty; of another, Sickness; of another, Sorrow; of the last, Sin. In one of these faculties we must be inscribed; the searching examination of one of these teachers we must pass before we can obtain our degree as Learned in the Art of Life.

Of most persons it may, perhaps, be said, without exaggeration, that they have a feeling of duty rather than a knowledge of it. When a certain situation present itself they tend to act in a certain way, but they cannot clearly state the principle or rule which determines their action. The business of the moral teacher is to clarify, to classify, and to enrich the content of the conscience.

LIFE AND DESTINY

We cannot demonstrate the existence of disinterester motives. The sole fact that we demand unselfishnests in action assures us that the standard of enlightened self-interest is false. And, indeed, if we consult the opinions of men where they are least likely to be warped by sophistry, w shall find that disinterestedness is the universal criterion by which moral worth is measured. If we suspect the motive we condemn the act.

LOVE AND MARRIAGE

LOVE is the expression of two natures in such fashion that each includes the other, each is enriched by the other.

Love is an echo in the feelings of a unity subsisting between two persons which is founded both on likeness and on complementary differences. Without the likeness there would be no attraction; without the challenge of the complementary differences there could not be the closer interweaving and the inextinguishable mutual interests which is the characteristic of all deeper relationships.

In the companionship of marriage our worth is tested. In that close and intimate relationship faults are inexorably laid bare, and virtues become doubly resplendent.

The fairest tribute that can be paid to a wife by a husband is that the love she inspires becomes stronger and deeper in the lapse of time; that nearness serves to heighten respect, and familiarity to enhance affection; and that each year, as it passes, but adds another gem to her crown as a wife and mother.

The spiritual quality of love transfigures the passions, transforms the fleeting fancy into a constant and growing attachment, the passing romance into a story without end, the interest of which never flags.

LIFE AND DESTINY

Unity of life is the keynote of love; the continuous blending of two into one lends to love its noble beauty, its divine significance.

Marriage is fundamentally holy because it is the foundation of homes. All the humanities have their origin in the home. All the virtues draw from it their nourishment. The human race is distinguished from the rest of the creation by the possession of homes.

The home is not built of brick and stone. It is a "temple not raised with hands." A man may live in a palace, furnished with all that wealth can afford or luxury invent. He may have at his command books, servants, troops of friends, and yet there may be a void in his life which tells him that he is homeless.

And what is the home feeling—if we consider the partners of the wedded life for a moment, apart from their offspring? It is the blessed sense of safety that comes to him who feels that he is rooted in another's affection, the sense of mutual protection, of mutual care and kindness, in sickness and in health, in good and in evil fortune, in life and close to the gates of death. Where the wife is, there is the home; and where the husband is, on land or sea. Oh, what a glad feeling it is to have one's own hearth! As the hearth gives warmth to the house, so marriage supplies an undiminishing inner warmth to those who partake of its blessings in the right spirit.

Marriage is the fountain upon which the tree of humanity depends for its life. If the fountain be pure

LOVE AND MARRIAGE

the tree will flourish and bear wholesome fruit. If the fountain be poisoned the tree must perish.

The god of Love is a jealous god. This does not mean that love should be wholly concentrated upon one person, but rather that the god of Love is jealous of anything in the heart that is not akin to love—jealous of hate, jealous of meanness, jealous of low and sordid aims.

The love of husband and wife is an epitome of every other kind of love. There is included in it something of the same feeling that brothers and sisters entertain for each other. There is a maternal element in the wife's feeling for the husband, and something of the fatherly spirit in the attitude of the husband toward the wife. And there is besides something more which is inexplicable and ineffable.

There are fundamental differences which distinguish the sexes in their mental and moral make-up, and marriage is designed to bring about the correlation of these differences, the mutual adaptation and reconciliation of them in a higher unity.

The present tendency to accentuate the qualities in which the sexes are alike is a temporary reaction against unjust discrimination in the past in favour of men. The differences are more important than the similarities, and ere long they will again receive the preponderant attention which is due to them.

One of the finest results of the further development of the human race will be the increasing differentiation of the sexes, leading to ever new, ever more complex, ever more exquisite reciprocal adjustments in the organisation of the wedded life.

The modern advocates of the elevation of women seem to be fundamentally mistaken in so far as they rely on the use of force—political or economic—for the attainment of their ends. Woman has secured her elevation in the past, and has immensely contributed toward moralising the human race, by precisely the opposite method; namely, by teaching men that there are certain rights which they must respect, though these rights cannot be enforced; that there are certain rights which men must respect on penalty of losing their self-respect.

It is the voice of tradition, the voice of humanity, the conscience of mankind pregnant with implicit truths which it may be impossible ever to make wholly explicit, that speaks from the lips of wives and mothers.

This I take to be the service which the wife can render the husband—she teaches him to submit to a law which is not sanctioned by force; and, in matters of the intellect, as well as of the character, she is his critic and his guide—not by a formulated code, but by the things she approves of or disapproves of.

The wife is just the one woman in the world who best performs for her husband these high offices. She helps him to decipher his soul, to gain self-knowledge—the most difficult kind of knowledge—to discover what qualities are latent in him; she reads his defects in the light of his possible excellence; she spurs him on to his

LOVE AND MARRIAGE

best performance; sustains him by her faith when he fails; and when he succeeds and gains the world's applause helps him to rate it at its proper worth, and to aspire toward aims that rise beyond the common approbation. And the husband, in turn, renders a corresponding service to the wife.

Only those who are linked together in the lifelong companionship of monogamic marriage Can thus serve one another. Apart from the interests of offspring, the spiritual interests of the wedded pair themselves demand that the union shall be a permanent one.

We are not married on our wedding-day; on that day we do but begin to be married. The true marriage is an endless process, the perpetual interlinking of two souls while life lasts.

A woman should be a home-keeper, but she should also go out from her home. She should take part in the struggle of society to create new and better conditions in politics, in social life, in religion. The real home-keeper should be in touch with the larger life of the world, in order that she may bring the breath of larger interests into her life, in order that she may open the windows of her house and let in the fresh breezes of the intellectual world around her. The finest, highest conception of a modern mother is that of one who trains the growing generation to take their places in the new world which is at present in the making, and how can she do this unless she herself carries the. new world in her heart, is receptive to the great ideas that are struggling to be, and comprehends them?

LIFE AND DESTINY

Marriage is an estate in which we seek to help each other to solve the total problem of our lives. The attraction of the sexes, seen in the light of this conception, is glorified and transfigured. Marriage is an estate in which we charge ourselves, not only with the comfort and the happiness of another, but with the problem of the total spiritual destiny of another. And because we live in our influence, because our life is strongest and purest where our influence is most penetrating, therefore in the estate of marriage it is possible for us to attain a depth of spiritual development such as can be achieved in no other human relationship whatsoever.

HIGHER LIFE

Let us earnestly strive to ascertain in what direction our strength lies, in order that we may become still stronger, and at what points we are weak, in order that we may fortify them, to the end that we may obey, however partially, the greatest of the commandments, "Be ye therefore perfect."

In general, the higher life may be characterised as the life which postpones the private to the public good, which is swayed by principles rather than impulses, and which bears testimony to the reality of the supreme ideals.

Man is like a tree, with the mighty trunk of intellect, the spreading branches of imagination, and the roots of the lower instincts that bind him to the earth. The moral life, however, is the fruit he bears; in it his true nature is revealed.

It is the prerogative of man that he need not blindly follow the law of his natural being, but is himself the author of a higher moral law, and creates it even in acting it out.

The higher life includes not only such virtues as personal purity, truthfulness, and a forgiving spirit toward enemies, but also embraces our obligations toward the State. No one can be, in the full sense, a good man who is not a good citizen.

LIFE AND DESTINY

There is a difficulty in the way of teaching the higher life, due to the fact that only those who have begun to lead it can understand the meaning of it. Nevertheless, all men can be induced to begin to lead it. Thought they seem blind, their eyes can be opened so as to see. Deep down in every human heart is the seed of a divine life, which only needs the quickening influence of right conditions to germinate.

It may be impossible for a man by merely willing it to add wings to his body, but it is possible for any man, by merely willing it, to add wings to his soul. This perennial miracle of the moral nature is capable of happening at any time.

An ideal is a port toward which we resolve to steer. We may not reach it. The mere fact that our goal is definitely located does not suffice to conduct us thither. But surely we shall thus stand a better chance of making port in the end than if we drift about aimlessly, the sport of winds and tides, without having decided in our own minds in what direction we ought to bend our course.

The moral law is the expression of our inmost nature, and when we live in consonance with it we feel that we are living out our true being.

The authority of conscience is founded on human nature itself. The imperative, which we cannot disown, comes from within. The distinction between right and wrong is as aboriginal as that between the true and the false. But whence shall we derive the strength to do the right and shun the wrong? What feelings are there which, in default of the hope of happiness and the fear of punishment in another world, and apart from the penalties of human legislation, shall sustain us in the struggle against evil? I believe that the fear of self-condemnation and the desire for self-respect can, by appropriate training, be so strengthened as to serve our purpose. For what man is there among all our friends and acquaintances whose opinion we have reason so greatly to dread as the opinion of the man within the man—our own self, namely, sitting in judgment upon us?

Among those who acknowledge the obligation of the moral law there are two classes—the class of moral bondmen and the class of moral freeman. Among the former belong those who recognise the particular moral commandments, but fail to recognise the unifying principle from which they flow; who see the satisfactions of which morality deprives them and the pains which it imposes, but fail to see the superior satisfactions to which obedience opens the way, and the ineffable peace that comes after the pain. Duty is a burden and a bondage to those who fix their attention only upon the negative aspect of it. It is a source of exaltation, despite the sufferings with which it is complicated, to those who firmly keep in view the positive aspect of it.

The "great occasions," morally speaking, are those that add to our strength by the very magnitude of the calls they make upon us, and that flatter our self-esteem by the dramatic incidents which are apt, at such critical moments, to attend the struggle against evil; but it cannot be too forcibly stated that the higher life, as a rule, must be led on the level of everyday existence, where the temptations to be resisted are commonplace and the petty details of duty seem to deprive the effort we put forth of all dignity and grandeur. Whether, under such circumstances, we shall be able to save our souls alive depends entirely on our point of view, on our bearing in mind that no detail of conduct is petty if it serves to exemplify a great principle.

In seeking for the highest good I cannot separate my quest so far as it concerns myself from the same quest so far as it concerns others. On the way to the highest goal I must take my fellow-beings with me. For the higher life—the germ of which exists in every man—is adequately represented by no man. The one represents more adequately some particular aspect of it, another a different aspect of it. It follows, therefore, that no one can love the higher life unless he seeks to promote it in others as well as in himself. All the so-called duties flow from the principle of the unity and interdependence of humanity in their effort toward the attainment of their goal.

The supreme ethical rule may be stated as follows: So act as to elicit the latent spiritual possibilities in others, and thereby in thyself. The aim definitely in view should be to influence others. Not one's own interests, not even one's own spiritual interests, should be in the foreground of consciousness. Yet we can in no wise draw out what is best in others without constantly renewing ourselves, making ourselves better fitted to exercise regenerative influence, and thus attaining the highest mental and moral growth of which we are

HIGHER LIFE

capable. This, it seems to me, is the true harmonising of opposites, this the point of view that reconciles the ever-conflicting claims of individualism and altruism. Not the good of self as a thing apart is the aim, nor the good of others as a thing apart, but a higher, over-arching good, to promote which is alike the highest good of self and others.

As light is light when it strikes on objects, so life is life when it smites on other life. We live truly in our radiations. We grow and develop in proportion as we help others to grow and develop.

The question of paramount importance, therefore, to be kept ever before the mind, is this: How, as a matter of fact, am I influencing the persons with whom I am in contact? How, as an employer, am I influencing my employees? How, as a citizen, am I influencing my fellow-citizens? How does the effect of my personality tell on wife and children and friends? Am I supremely interested in getting the best results out of the people with whom I am in touch? Am I helping them to make the most of themselves?

There are certain obvious marks of the higher life. One is Purity. This does not mean that the senses shall be suppressed, but that the inferior part of our nature shall be taken up into the superior, the senses wedded to the soul.

A second mark of the higher life is Serenity, and there is perhaps no surer sign by which exalted natures can be known. To be serene under all circumstances whatsoever, even in moments of imminent peril, in times of sudden reversal of fortune, of grievous personal loss or of public calamity, is the unmistakable badge of moral ripeness. But is it possible to preserve one's serenity in the supreme trials of life? It is possible, I should answer, if we have formed the habit of asking on every occasion, what is it right to do now? The habit of fixing our attention on how we are to conduct ourselves, on what, in a given situation and quite apart from our feelings, it is right to do, steadies the pulse, clears the eye and preserves the tranquility of the soul. And there is always something which it is right to do, even in the most desperate circumstances, if it be only to maintain our dignity as human beings, to keep up the drooping spirits of those around us, and to assist our weaker brethren to the last.

Another token of the higher life, which indeed is implied in the former, is the habit of taking what is called an objective or impersonal view of our personal relations. This is especially important as helpful to self-control. We are at best but tyros in the art of living, so long as we continue to give effect in our dealings with others to our mere personal antipathies and sympathies. As soon as we learn to speak and act medicinally, not from personal resentment or under the impulse of personal attraction, but with a view to promoting just the good in others, the whole atmosphere in which we breathe changes; a kind of perpetual sunshine illuminates our inner world, the clouds of hate and the mists of passionate feeling dissolve and peace reigns within the borders of the soul.

HIGHER LIFE

A fourth token of the higher life is Wisdom. Wisdom is situated at the junction of the intellectual and the moral faculties. It consists in the highest use of the intellect for the discernment of the largest moral interests of humanity. It is the most perfect willingness to do the right combined with the utmost attainable knowledge of what is right, and with the clearest perception of what, in a given situation, is feasible. Wisdom is the attribute of one who works toward the most sublime ends imaginable, but who at the same time realises the limitations due to existing conditions and who, free from impatience at the unavoidable imperfections of man's estate, seeks to achieve the better as a step leading in the direction of the best. Wisdom consists in working for the better from the love of the best. The world is full of reformers who thunder at the gates of the Impossible, seeking to force an entrance, and who injure their causes, as well as themselves, by the inevitable reaction which ensues when their schemes are found to be impracticable. Wisdom teaches that it is possible to lead the higher life, even now.

But the crowning grace of all is Humility, in the sense in which it implies and presupposes dignity. Dignity is based upon the consciousness of a divine element in human nature, of an infinite aim, a boundless destiny. Humbleness is due to a sense of the incalculable distance which still separates us from the goal. These two, inseparably combined, are the invariable accompaniment of moral greatness wherever met with. Self-righteousness and a cynical contempt of human nature

LIFE AND DESTINY

on the other hand are the two chief enemies of moral progress. These monsters must be slain if we would hope to continue in the upward path.

The higher life cannot be attained without rigorous self-discipline, and self-discipline always involves pain, but the end in view is worthy of the sufferings we are called upon to endure, the prize is worthy of the price exacted of us.

SPIRITUAL PROGRESS

By what sort of experience are we led to the conviction that spirit exists? On the whole, by searching, painful experience. The rose Religion grows on a thornbush, and we must not be afraid to have our fingers lacerated by the thorns if we would pluck the rose. For instance, a person who endures great bodily suffering with fortitude will discover that there is something in him which physical agony cannot overcome, something not of the senses, which all the assaults of the senses are powerless to affect.

Why in this world of ours there should be so much suffering no one knows. But this we know; that, evil existing, the world being such as it is, we can win from evil, if we choose, an inestimable good, namely—the conviction that there is in us a power not of the senses, the conviction that spirit exists, and exists in us.

A skeptic may say that in a world ideally conceiveable we might have secured this precious conviction without the necessity of undergoing the ordeal of pain. To which the reply is: that in a world ideally conceiveable what he says may be true; but in the world as it is, with which alone we are concerned, we have ample cause for gratitude that we can turn suffering to such far-reaching account, that we can distill from the bitter root this divine elixir; that by manfully bearing the pains of the senses, inexplicable though they be, we are able to gain the certainty that a power not born of the senses exists in us, operates in us. It is this effect of pain that accounts for the serenity and peace of many patient sufferers, a peace and a serenity which surround their bed of misery with a kind of halo.

The same is true of moral pain. The experience of guilt, for instance, if it leads us to pitilessly honest self-scrutiny and self-judgment, will at the last disclose the marvelous fact that even in the most desperate cases there remains a part of our nature unspoiled by guilt. We become aware of a power within us, to slough off the guilt as the serpent sloughs off its skin; to triumph over the evil we have done as well as over the evils we suffer. We realize that there is in us a fount of indexhaustella moral rejuvenation.

What, then, are the compensations of sin? In the first place, a truer insight into the moral order of the universe, a more adequate realization of the authority of those holy ordinances against which we have offended; and then the conviction that the soul can ever rise again by its own efforts. The tree may fall, but the root remains indestructible; the spring of moral endevour may appear to be dried up, but there are hidden subterranean streams from which it can ever be fed anew.

The stages of the progress of mankind may be compared to a series of mountain ranges. First the foothills, then the higher hills, then mountain range on mountain range beyond them. As we gain the loftier eminences we see the snowy summits before us, touched by the light of the moral ideal, transforming themselves before our eyes into what appear to be the ramparts and spires of the Golden City. We climb still higher, and the vision travels with us, lighting on the next succeeding range. And so, on and on, as we ascend.

We live in our activities, in our influence. The success or failure of life is determined, not by our conditions, but by the effort we put forth despite our Conditins. A man who, though himself poor, labors to keep alive the higher life in his fellows, to inspire them with the courage to strive for the better, and with patience to bear the evils which are for the time being unavoidable, is a spiritual hero and a nobler benefactor than many of the so-called benefactors who invade the slums.

When human nature fights in the last ditch, when it is pressed against the wall, when the clutch of cir-substances is about its throat and threatens to choke it, then human nature, by way of reaction, exhibits a power which we call spiritual. This is rarely displayed in prosporous circumstances. It is the compensation of adversity that it elicits in manifold ways this spiritual power and makes man's life in a spiritual sense a success.

SUFFERING AND CONSOLATION

LET the Stoics say what they will, so long as we remain human we shall always open our breasts to those warm loves that make the sweetness of existence, if also they make its bitterest pain.

It is written that the last enemy to be vanquished is death. We should begin early in life to vanquish this enemy by obliterating every trace of the fear of death from our minds. Then can we turn to life and fill the whole horizon of our souls with it, turn with added zest to all the serious tasks which it imposes and to the pure delights which here and there it affords.

There are hours of great loneliness, when the frost of desolation penetrates into the very soul, when the burden seems too heavy to bear, and the draught of life too bitter to swallow. But the very keenness of the ordeal begets the strength to bear it, and patience and unselfish resignation will come as with the rustling of angels' wings to dry our scalding tears.

When the light of the sun shines through a prism it is broken into beautiful colors, and when the prism is shattered, still the light remains. So does the light of life shine resplendent in the forms of our friends, and so, when their forms are broken, still their life remains; and in that life we are united with them; for the life of their life is also our life, and we are one with them by ties indissoluble.

SUFFERING AND CONSOLATION

They say that it is a blessed relief in times of grief to shed tears. But a more blessed relief than to shed tears is to wipe away the tears from others' eyes.

In hours of great sorrow we turn in vain to Nature for an inspiring thought. We question the sleepless stars; they are cold and distant. The winds blow, the rivers run their course, the seasons change; they are careless of man. Only in the human world do we find an answering echo to our needs.

The body is incapable of supporting for longer than a few brief years the weight of the life that dwells within it. The vehicle cannot sustain the content. The instrument falls short of the demands upon it, and crumbles into ruins. But in its ruin it sets off, in tragic contrast, the grandeur of the power which, for a time, employed it for its uses, a power greater than itself, greater than any instrument, whose glory rises above the ruins and gilds them with unearthly splendor in departing.

We are soldiers fighting a good fight. The call that awakens us out of despair in times of affliction is the trumpet-call of duty, summoning us back to the battle.

The experience of progress in the past, the hope of progress toward perfection in the future, is the redeeming feature of life; it is the one and only solace that never fails.

It is the nature of the noble and the good and the wise that they impart to us of their nobility and their goodness and their wisdom while they live, making it

LIFE AND DESTINY

natural for us to breathe the air they breathe and giving us confidence in our own untested powers. And the same influence in more ethereal fashion they continue to exert after they are gone.

The condition of all progress is experience. We go wrong a thousand times before we find the right path. We struggle, and grope, and hurt ourselves until we learn the use of things, and this is true of things spiritual as well of material things. Pain is nevoidable, but it acquires a new and higher meaning when we perceive that it is the price humanity must pay for an invaluable good.

The consolations of the moral ideal are vigorous. They do not encourage idle sentiment. They recommend to the sufferer action. Our loss, indeed, will always remain loss, and no preaching or teaching can ever make it otherwise. But the question is whether it shall weaken and embitter, or strengthen and purify us and lead us to raise to the dead we mourn a monument in our lives that shall be better than any pillared chapel or storied marble tomb.

The criterion of all right relations whatsoever is that we are helped by them. And so, too, the criterion of right relations to the dead is that we are helped, not weakened and disabled, by them. Does the rimebrace of our departed beloved ones have this effect upon us? Does it make us better and purer men and women than we should otherwise have been, stronger if not happier? Do they come to us as gentle monitors in silent hours of thought? Does their approving smile

SUFFERING AND CONSOLATION

stimulate us to greater bravery for the right, to more earnest self-conquest? Does the pressure of their investbile hands guide us in the better way? If so, then truly blessed is their memory. Then will the pain which is associated with the thought of them gradually be diminished; the wild regrets, the unappeasable longings which, at times, assert themselves gradually be pacified. Then will the bitter sense of the loss we have sustained be overborne by the consciousness of the treasure of their influence which still remains to us, and which can never be taken from us.

Activity is our great resource. To be active is to live. The glow that comes with activity supplies the heat that supports our mental and moral energies. Activity is the antidote to the depressions that lower our vitality, whether they come from physical or psychical causes.

Those whom we love are not given to us merely for our joy or our happiness. Their truest ministry consists in being to us revealers of the divine. They quicken in us the seed of better thoughts, help us to estimate rightly the things that are worth trying for and the things that are not worth trying for; help us to become more equal to the standard of our own best insight, and grow into our truer selves. And this influx- once abides when they are gone.

Let us learn from the lips of death the lessons of life. Let us live truly while we live, live for what is true and good and lasting. And let the memory of our dead help us to do this. For they are not wholly sepal-rated from us, if we remain loyal to them. In spirit they are with us. And we may think of them as silent, invisible, but real presences in our households.

In a storm at sea when the peril is extreme, the captain lashes himself to the mast in order that he may bring the vessel safely through the raging seas. So, in times of great affliction, we should lash ourselves to the mast of the ship of life, by the cord of duty.

The bitter, yet merciful, lesson which death teaches us is to distinguish the gold from the tinsel, the true values from the worthless chaff.

The terrible events of life are great eye-openers. They force us to learn that which it is wholesome for us to know, but which habitually we try to ignore—namely, that really we have no claim on a long life; that we are each of us liable to be called off at any moment, and that the main point is not how long we live, but with what meaning we fill the short allotted span—for short it is at best.

The wine of pleasure which once we quaffed so passionately, where is it now? The cup is empty and only the lees remain, and they are as wormwood to the taste. The flowers which we move into chaplets at our feasts to wreathe ourselves withal, they are withered and noxious. But the good deeds we have done, the nobler traits of character we have developed—these are imperishable.

As in every battle, so in the great battle of Hubmunity, the fallen and wounded, too, have a share in the victory; by their sufferings they have helped, and the greenest wreaths belong to them.

SUFFERING AND CONSOLATION

We conceive of ourselves as somehow identical in being with those who are to come after us; for it is in the nature of spirit that its separate members, diesparsed though they be in space and time, are still, in essence, one. So that we may say concerning those who come after us, and who will reap the benefit of our labors, that we ourselves shall attain to increasing per faction in them.

All of us have felt after some great bereavement the beneficent influence of mere work. Even the mechemical part of our daily tasks affords us some relief. The knowledge that something must be done prevents us from brooding over our grief's, and forces us back into the active currents of life.

The resources of the intellect, too, stand us in good stead in times of trouble. The pursuit of knowedge is directed toward large impersonal ends: into the calm and silent realm of thought the feelings can gain no entrance. There, after the first spasms of emotion have subsided, we may find at least a temporary relief —there for hours we drink in a welcome oblivion. But mere plodding toil and mere intellectual preoccupypotion do not suffice, the discharge of the moral duties in the light of the moral perfection to which they point alone can really sustain and console us.

In alleviating the misery of others our own misery will be alleviated; in healing there is cure.

When we endure some heavy affliction we are apt to say, "Oh, there is no suffering like my suffering. There is no one who bears such a load as mine." This is a mistake—the guilty suffer more than the afflicted.

LIFE AND DESTINY

Better a thousand times death than shame. There are depths below depths, abysses below abysses.

Poverty, sickness, sorrow, and the experience of sin are the great instrumentalities for moralizing our natures. They are dark gateways through which we pass into a temple of light—into the innermost sankteary of a truer life. Yes, for the guilty also there is consolation and redemption. "Come ye that are heavy laden unto me, no matter how heavily laden with sin." says every religion, "and I will give you rest." For those who have transgressed the moral law realize more fully than others do the sublime majesty of the power which they have affronted. And in a sense greater than words can convey, those who have had the profoundest experience of guilt are more capable than others of a divine transfiguration of their natures.

We are not free to stand aside in idle woe, but should make for the departed a memorial in our lives and complete their half-completed tasks. The widowed wife shall be both mother and father to her children; the afflicted husband both father and mother to his children.

Faith in the sublime ideal of humanity is the saving faith that will work miracles today, as of old at Cana, that will change the waters of earth's grief and misery into the wondrous wine of life and joy.

Death and the dead should be associated with what is brightest and purest in nature, with glorious sunsets, with the dawn of summer mornings, with the fragrance of spring.

ETHICAL OUTLOOK

The right for the right's sake is the motto which every one should take for his own life. With that as a standard of value we can descend into our hearts, appraise ourselves, and determine how far we already are moral beings, how far not yet.

The supremacy of the moral end of life above-all other ends, the sufficiency of man for the pursuit of that end, the increase of moral truth to be expected from loyalty in this pursuit—these are the three tenets, if we may call them so, of an ethical creed.

The question what to believe is perhaps the most momentous that any one can put to himself. Our beliefs are not to be classed among the luxuries, but among the necessaries of existence. They become particularly important in times of trouble. They are like the life-boats carried by ocean ships. As long as the sea is smooth and there is every appearance of a prosperous voyage, the passengers seldom take note of the boats or inquire into their sea-worthiness. But when the storm breaks and danger approaches, then the capacity of the boats and their soundness become matters of the first importance.

Ethical religion affirms the continuity of progress toward moral perfection. It affirms that the spiritual development of the human race cannot be prematurely cut off, either gradually or suddenly; that every stone of offence against which we stumble is a stepping-stone to some greater good; that, at the end of days, if we choose to put it so, all the rays of progress will be summed and centered in a transcendent focus.

Religion is concerned with the foreign relations of mankind, that is to say, with our relations to the whole of outside nature. The mission of religion is to convince us that the foreign power is friendly. The non-ethical religions have represented the eternal outside power as manifesting its friendliness by warding off unhappiness and ministering to the temporal well-being of man. Ethical religion restricts itself to affirming that the eternal power assures the fulfillment of our moral aims. The non-ethical religions have based the belief that there is a higher power on the testimony of supernatural revelations. Ethical religion bases its belief solely upon the testimony of conscience, which declares that progress ought to be achieved, hence inferring that it will be.

That the moral obligation remains in force is the capital fact to which we must hold fast, no matter what may be our theories of life and the universe. The recognition of this obligation, the hearty avowal of the supremacy of the moral end above all other ends of life, is the first article of a practical ethical creed.

There may be, and there ought to be, progress in the moral sphere. The moral truths which we have inherited from the past need to be expanded and restated.

ETHICAL OUTLOOK

In times of misfortune we require for our support something of which the truth is beyond all question, in which we can put an implicit trust, "though the heavens should fall." A merely borrowed belief is, at such times, like a rotten plank across a raging torrent. The moment we step upon it, it gives way beneath our feet.

Good deeds remain good, no matter whether we know how the world was made or not. Vile deeds are vile, no matter whether we know or do not know what, after death, will be the fate of the doer. We know, at least, what his fate is now, namely, to be wedded to the vileness.

The question for any one to decide, who hesitates between good and evil, is whether he aspires to be a full-weight man, or merely the fragment, nay, the counterfeit of a man. Only he who ceaselessly aims at moral completeness is, in the true sense, a human being.

There is a universal element in man which he can assert by so acting as if the purpose of the universe were also his purpose. It is the function of the supreme ordeals of life to develop in men this power, to give to their life this distinction, this height of dignity, these vast horizons.

Life has ever seemed to me a task. It has its interludes of joy. But, on the whole, it is an arduous, often a desperately arduous task. I think of the dead as of those who have finished their task, who have graduated from this exacting school, who have taken their degree—and some of them, surely, with honour.

LIFE AND DESTINY

We need to feel that no effort is ever wasted, that no honest reaching out toward the good is vain, that the great All is pressing forward toward a transcendent goal. And there is but a single way to obtain this conviction. It is not possible to enter into the nature of the Good by standing aloof from it—by merely speculating upon it. Act the Good, and you will believe in it. Throw yourself into the stream of the world's good tendency and you will feel the force of the current and the direction in which it is setting. The conviction that the world is moving toward great ends of progress will come surely to him who is himself engaged in the work of progress.

By ceaseless efforts to live the good life we maintain our moral sanity. Not from without, but from within, flow the divine waters that renew the soul.

The ethical element of religion has ever been its truly vital and quickening force. It is this which lends such majesty to the speeches of the Prophets, which gives such ineffable power and sweetness to the words of Jesus. Has this ethical element become less important in our age? Has the need of accentuating it become less imperative?

Today, in the estimation of many, science and art are taking the place of religion. But science and art alike are inadequate to build up character and to furnish binding rules of conduct.

We need also a clearer understanding of applied ethics, a better insight into the specific duties of life, a finer and a surer moral tact.

ETHICAL OUTLOOK

It is the business of the preacher, not only to state moral truths, but to inspire his hearers with a realising sense of their value, and to awaken in them the desire to act accordingly. He can do this only by putting his own purpose as a yeast into their hearts. The influence of the right sort of preachers cannot be spared. The human race is not yet so far advanced that it can dispense with the impulses that come from men of more than average intensity of moral energy.

Let us produce, through the efficacy of a better moral life and of a deeper moral experience, a surer faith in the ultimate victory of the good.

Let us found religion upon a basis of perfect intellectual honesty. Religion, if it is to mean anything at all, must stand for the highest truth. How then can the cause of truth be served by the sacrifice, more or less disguised, of one's intellectual convictions?

To those who are longing for a higher life, who deeply feel the need of religious satisfactions, we suggest that there is a way in which the demands of the head and the heart may be reconciled. Religion is not necessarily allied with dogma, a new kind of faith is possible, based not upon legend and tradition, not upon the authority of any book, but upon the moral nature of man.

Theologians often say that faith must come first, and that morality must be deduced from faith. We say that morality must come first, and faith, to those whose nature fits them to entertain it, will come out of the experience of a deepened moral life as its richest, choicest fruit

Precisely because moral culture is the aim, we cannot be content merely to lift the mass of mankind above the grosser forms of evil. We must try to advance the cause of humanity by developing in ourselves, as well as in others, a higher type of manhood and womanhood than the past has known.

To aid in the evolution of a new conscience, to inject living streams of moral force into the dry veins of materialistic communities is our aim.

We seek to come into touch with the ultimate power of things, the ultimate peace in things, which yet, in any literal sense, we know well that we cannot know. We seek to become morally certain—that is, certain for moral purposes—of what is beyond the reach of demonstration. But our moral optimism must include the darkest facts that pessimism can point to, include them and transcend them.

To give to actual life the formal poise and finish of a work of art is the tendency of those who see in learning and beauty the highest end of human endeavor. It is a tendency the value of which as an element of wisdom cannot be denied; but it cannot, on the other hand, be said that it is "the religious teaching which is proper to our time." The watchword "culture" we may indeed adopt. But there is needed the qualifying prefix "ethical" to give it a practical direction and a higher than the merely aesthetic connotation.

ETHICAL OUTLOOK

We should teach our children nothing which they shall ever need to unlearn; we should strive to transmit to them the best possessions, the truest thought, the noblest sentiments of the age in which we live.

The moral ferment that has worked from the beginning in human nature is active still. Today it is manifest in the great social problems that agitate our age, demanding a higher justice, if they are to be solved, threatening social disruption if they are met in the hard spirit of selfish greed, while promising a fairer future than the world has yet seen if dealt with in wisdom and forbearance.

The frontier of the higher life is everywhere contiguous to the common life, and we can cross the border at any moment. The higher life is as real as the grosser things in which we put our trust. But our eyes must be anointed so that we may see it.

The office of the religious teacher is to be a seer, and to make others see, and thus to win them into the upward way.

They have not grasped the whole truth who see in the sympathetic side of human nature, in the tender and amiable impulses of the heart, the well-spring of our moral judgments. These gentle qualities—pity, tenderness, sympathy—are the sweet, younger sisters of Virtue; but Virtue herself is greater than they.

We should seek to free the moral life from the embarrassments and entanglements in which it has been involved by the quibbles of the schools and the mutual antagonisms of the sects; to introduce into it an element of downrightness and practical earnestness; above all, to secure to the modern world, in its struggle with manifold evil, the boon of moral unity, despite intellectual diversity.

In order to improve ethics as a science it is necessary to fix attention on the moral facts, to collect them, to bring them into view, especially the more recondite facts.

Many of us stumble, not because we lack the desire to do what is right, but because we fail to discern what the right is.

I believe in the supreme excellence of righteousness; I believe that the law of righteousness will triumph in the universe over all evil; I believe that in the attempt to fulfill the law of righteousness, however imperfect, it must remain, are to be found the inspiration, the consolation, and the sanctification of human existence.

We live in order to finish an, as yet, unfinished universe, unfinished so far as the human, that is, the highest part of it, is concerned. We live in order to develop the superior qualities of man which are, as yet, for the most part latent.

The test of genuine moral culture is to be found in the attention we pay to the oft-neglected details of conduct; in the extent to which we have formed the habit of asking, What is it right to do in those little things which yet are not little?

The thought of the brevity of life is the prod that spurs us on to the achievement of our task; it is like

ETHICAL OUTLOOK

the blast of a bugle from the walls of a fortress that warns us to make haste lest the gates be closed against us.

We are to go out as teachers among the people, discarding the limitations imposed by the theologies of the past, and holding up the moral ideal, pure and simple, as the human ideal, as the ideal for all men, embracing all men, binding on all men—the ideal of a perfect society, of a society in which no men or class of men shall be mere hewers of wood and drawers of water for others; in which no man or woman, or class of men or class of women shall be used as tools for the lusts of others, or for the ambitions of others, or for the greed of others; in which every human life, the life of every man and woman and child, shall be esteemed a sacred utterance of the Infinite.

THE AMERICAN ETHICAL UNION is a national association of Societies for Ethical Culture. It is devoted to the promotion of the knowledge, the love and the practice of the right in all the relationships of life. It affirms the simple belief that the greatest spiritual values are to be found in man's relationship to man. Through its religious and educational programs it seeks to make the individual more adequate in his personal relationships and better able to contribute to the life of his community.

There are Ethical Societies and Fellowships in the following communities:

BALTIMORE, MARYLAND
BERGEN COUNTY, NEW JERSEY
BOSTON, MASSACHUSETTS
BROOKLYN, NEW YORK
CHICAGO, ILLINOIS
CLEVELAND, OHIO
ESSEX COUNTY, NEW JERSEY
LAKELAND, WAYNE, NEW JERSEY
LITTLE ROCK, ARKANSAS
GARDEN CITY, L.I., NEW YORK
LOS ANGELES, CALIFORNIA
NORTH MIAMI BEACH, FLORIDA
MONMOUTH COUNTY, NEW JERSEY
NEW YORK, NEW YORK
NORTHERN WESTCHESTER, NEW YORK
PHILADELPHIA, PENNSYLVANIA
QUEENS, NEW YORK
RESTON, VIRGINIA
RIVERDALE-YONKERS, NEW YORK
SAN DIEGO, CALIFORNIA
ST. LOUIS, MISSOURI
SUFFOLK, LONG ISLAND, NEW YORK
WASHINGTON, D. C.
WESTCHESTER COUNTY, NEW YORK

For addresses of Ethical Societies and Fellowship Groups and information about the Member-At-Large program write to: American Ethical Union, 2 West 64th Street, New York, New York 10023∎

www.ingramcontent.com/pod-product-compliance
Lightning Source LLC
Chambersburg PA
CBHW071749040426
42446CB00012B/2502